C000102874

Contents:

Hudson Taylor

The Missionary Who Won a Nation by Prayer

1832—1905

Great men and women are not in need of our praise.
We are the ones in need of getting to know them.

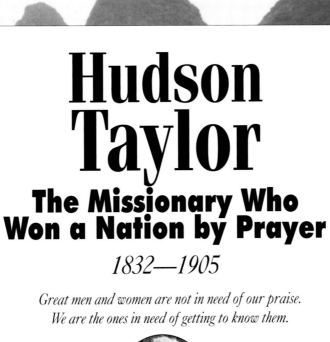

By Marlee Alex

Illustrations by Giuseppe Rava

Scandinavia

STORM AT SEA

A tall, thin figure stood at the rail of a wooden ship looking toward the open water. I can't wait to get to China, the young man thought. Shivers of excitement ran down his spine. Lord, put the wind at our backs. Move this ship on toward the East. In the wind I can almost hear the cries of the Chinese people. They've never heard the Word of God or the name of Jesus. I'm going into the interior of that huge empire and will be the first Protestant missionary to bring them the message of salvation. Blow wind, go on and blow us toward China.

The morning wore on, and as the man stood by the railing and paced the deck, the sea grew rougher. His prayers for a safe voyage seemed to have been lost in the foam of the wild waves. Finally he fought his way to the captain on the bridge. Waves towered over the crew of men working the rigging on deck. Cold water smashed against the bow with hurricane force, nearly splintering the timbers and threatening to drag the sailors into the ocean depths.

"How far have we come from the coast?" he shouted above the crash of the sea.

Captain Morris was fighting with the sail and listening for any sign or sound that the wood was cracking. His ship, called the Dumfries, leaned at an incline down toward the black-gray water, then rebounded and clipped along the sea's surface at lightning speed. "Not far," Morris shouted back. "This is the worst storm I've ever seen. We're heading toward a rocky beach wall. I can't turn her!"

The young man crawled below, slamming into the walls and furniture in his cabin as the ship rocked back and forth. He fished out a pen from the desk, and clearly scribbled his

4

name – HUDSON TAYLOR — into a notebook, then fastened this securely inside his pocket. Perhaps this way when they find my body, they can identify it for my parents, Taylor thought. He wrestled with his fear and was already grieving the loss of his dream — to bring the Gospel of Jesus Christ to those living in the interior of China.

Years of preparation buried at sea, he thought. All I've worked for, gone. He climbed back up to the slippery deck.

There, Hudson saw right away that the ship, rocking and plunging in the wilderness of water, was already within two ship's lengths of a jagged rock near the shore. Captain Morris was heaving at the sail like a wild man. Taylor grabbed hold of a thick rope and held on. Will I never see China, he thought. Will this be the end of my dream? In the bone-chilling chaos he relived the history of that dream and brought to mind childhood memories of his home in Barnsley, England . . . .

CHILDHOOD MEMORIES

"**Y**ou're late again, Hudson!" his father, James Taylor, exclaimed.

The five-year-old boy shuddered as he climbed into his place at the table between his two sisters. He knew that being late for meals was never tolerated. But Mr. Taylor merely said, "It won't happen again, will it son?"

"No, father," Hudson replied.

"Now, let us thank God for this food. Then after lunch Hudson, you and I will go and work an hour at the pharmacy, then begin our Latin lessons before tea. You'll have it ready, my dear Amelia?"

There were times when Hudson grew tired of his parents' stringent rules, but he still adored his father and mother. Through them he found security and love beyond the orderli-

ness they demanded.

Hudson's home was full of warmth: the tidy parlor with its glowing oil lamps, crumpets and shortbread at the tea table, his father's head bowed over breakfast during long periods of prayer. Prayers always seemed to last far longer than Hudson's young, restless little body could endure. But in his father's shop, where pharmaceutical bottles of every color and description covered the shelves, Hudson's imagination was given full play. He liked watching his father mix, pound and wrap the different medicines for his customers.

During the afternoons Hudson's sisters, young Amelia and Louisa, sat beside him in home school, their eyebrows wrinkled as they studied languages, history and arithmetic. But the best times of all were during winter evenings by the coal fire. The voices of his parents and their friends would drone on and on over the chink of china tea cups and saucers. As a boy, Hudson often drifted into

sleep while listening to the adults talk about theology, politics and ministry within the Methodist church.

"Learn to love your Bible above all," Hudson's father frequently told him. "God cannot fail." Often he would lead his son to the tall bookcase with glass doors. Mr. Taylor would pull down one book after another, sometimes from a collection about the country of China. "Who invented gunpowder?" he would ask. "The compass? Paper? The art of printing? Which people of the earth live in an ancient empire over one hundred times the size of England?"

Hudson knew the answer every time. "The Chinese," he would say.

Now 21 years old, Hudson knelt on the deck of the tossing ship, and cried out to God for survival and safe passage to that nation he longed to see. Strengthened by his memories, he remembered the moment God had actually called him to China . . . .

HUDSON RECEIVES A CALLING

"Your dad's a right old religious fanatic!" one boy said to Hudson.

Hudson opened the Barnsley Bank books and began to add up the numbers and record the accounts. Although only 15, he was already living on his own and earning a living.

"All Christians are hypocrites," his friends continued. "You've got your own life to live, Hudson. Why go on with your father's old-fashioned God?"

Hudson pretended not to mind. But he was thinking, It's true, Dad's prayers and all that church language does seem so ridiculous! I'm so sick of it.

Yet Hudson could not free himself from the tug of God. He finally made his decision and told the boys, "I'll believe what I want to. God is the wisest course. He cannot fail."

In his own mind though, Hudson was afraid he might just be repeating his father's words. It's not my faith or my choice, he thought to himself.

Besides, church is a bore and I don't have to go there now that I'm not living at home anymore.

Hudson brooded, unsure of where he fit in. He wanted adventure and challenge, yet he felt unhappy whenever he imitated the other boys and went along with their pranks.

One afternoon when he was 17, Hudson wandered into his father's library, hoping to find a way to fill an empty afternoon. He picked up a gospel tract that appealed to him with the promise of an amusing story. I'll skip the sermon, he thought. I've heard them all a thousand times. But Hudson was wrong. The simple truth in the message of the story captured his attention. He didn't need the sermon; God was speaking to him personally, calling him to a lifetime of faith.

"Lord, I accept Jesus as my Savior," Hudson prayed that day. As months passed, certainty and vision replaced the confusion and turmoil he had felt.

But Hudson wasn't content just to go to church and be a Christian in name. He longed to do something daring. Something that had never been done before. "I will go anywhere, do anything, suffer anything for You, Lord," he prayed. "Please give me the assurance of what You want me to do."

As he prayed, he could almost feel God's presence. It was as if God was saying, "Your prayer is answered, your conditions accepted. I will call you to a rugged life that will be hard on your body and make you trust in Me, not any man."

Hudson believed God was calling him to China, the land that his father and mother loved to talk so much about. He decided to begin preparing immediately for missionary service. Hudson began to exercise his body and to evangelize among the poor in the worst areas of his own hometown. He visited the alleyways and marketplaces, passing out gospel tracts and preaching from the Bible. The more he spoke to others about Jesus, the more he felt at the center of God's will. But every day, he longed more and more to evangelize among the people who had never even heard the name of Jesus and where, in the interior of the country, there was not a single Protestant missionary to bring them the Good News.

Hudson knew China was closed to foreigners at that time and that the Taiping Rebellion, a kind of civil war, was in full swing. But these obstacles only made him that much more determined. He began to dream of the impossible. I will go, he thought. I will be the first to come with the message of salvation to the millions living deep in the heart of China.

Hudson took a job as a physician's assistant, hoping to use medicine and its practice as a way of getting inside China. In order to prepare himself for the cultural challenges of that land, he decided to move out of his own comfortable home and go live among the poor. He rented a cold, barely furnished apartment and gave up the diet he was used to. Refusing to live well while his neighbors suffered, he existed on only oatmeal or rice, a biscuit and herring, or a few apples a day. In his free time he visited the poor, bringing medicine, comfort

China's Political History

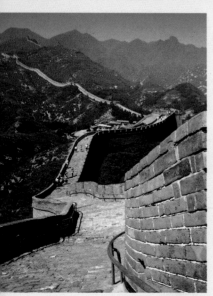

China is a country with a rich cultural heritage, stretching back to the dawn of civilization. After centuries of turmoil and fighting among local rulers, China rose out of prehistoric times as an empire of thirty six states, or provinces. The first emperor, Qin Shihuang (259-210 B.C.) built the famous Great Wall as a defense against the nomadic tribes to the north, and laid the foundation for what later became the world's greatest civilization

Caption: The Chinese Wall

during the next centuries.

Early in the thirteenth century China was overthrown by the Mongol empire and trade with Europe was promoted for the first time. The most famous European to visit China was the explorer Marco Polo, who returned to Europe and told about this highly civilized, rich country in the East. The Mongols were eventually driven out and the Ming Dynasty ruled China for 300 years until the Manchus invaded northern China in 1644. During the Manchu rule China opened up to European and American trade and influence.

from the Scriptures or prayers. And he always remembered to invite them into a relationship with Jesus Christ.

In 1840 a Manchu official burned a shipload of British-owned opium intended to be sold in China. War broke out between the two countries. England won and forced China to open some of its ports to European trade. The Europeans began to support the Manchu rulers against the Chinese peasants because the Manchus favored European business interests. The peasantsrevolted and the Taiping Rebellion broke out. The revolt was put down. But the Manchu Dynasty was weakened and in 1911 Chinese revolutionaries finally overthrew the imperial government and established a republic.

However, the Chinese people were not trained for democracy. Over the following years the country suffered under local military chiefs, or warlords, who fought each other for power. An exhausting war with Japan broke out in 1931 and continued until it became part of World War II. China then joined the Allies against Germany, Italy and Japan.

When the war was over, the Communists managed to take control of China, and in September 1949 a new Communist government was set up in Beijing, establishing the People's Republic of China, with Chairman Mao Zedong as its head. China is still ruled by Communist dictators today.

Caption: Mao Zedong proclaims the Communist Republic of China

THE LESSONS OF FAITH

One day the physician who employed Hudson forgot to pay him his wages. In fact, the man was so forgetful he had often asked Hudson to remind him to pay his wages every week. But Hudson had been wondering what more he could do to make sure he'd be ready to face life as a missionary. He decided to use his employer's forgetfulness as an occasion to trust God. I won't remind Dr. Hardey, he thought. I will just pray about money for my rent and food and train myself to put my expectations in the Lord instead of man.

Hudson discovered that putting his faith to the test was not an easy thing. One Sunday evening when Hudson had nothing but one coin left, a poor man approached him and asked if he would come to his home and pray with his wife, who was dying. Hudson asked the man why he had not called his own priest.

"I did," said the man, "but he

wouldn't come without payment and we haven't a cent to our name. My children are starving."

Hudson thought of the coin in his pocket, the only money he had. He thought of the last bowl of porridge and piece of bread waiting for him at his lodging. "How is it you have allowed your family to reach such a desperate state?" Hudson asked. "You should have called the civil authorities for help."

To himself Hudson thought, If only I had two coins, I'd give the man one

of them. The two men continued walking through the night, down into a courtyard, then up a tiny flight of stairs and into a wretched room. There Hudson saw five children sitting on the ground, their cheeks and temples sunken with hunger. Lying on the floor beside them was their mother with a tiny infant at her side. Hudson noticed that instead of crying, the baby seemed to be in exhausted pain. If only I had an extra coin, he thought. I would be happy to give it to them so they could buy food for the children.

"Don't be discouraged," Hudson said to the family. "You have a loving Father in Heaven who knows your needs."

But within him, Hudson heard a voice. "Hypocrite!" the voice said. "You tell these people to trust God, yet you are not willing to trust Him yourself without that money in your pocket!"

Hudson began to feel he was the one in need of comfort and help. "Let's pray together, shall we?" he asked.

But again, the voice spoke to his heart: "Are you mocking God, Hudson? Give that coin away!"

Hudson finished his prayer, looked into the eyes of the children, put his hand into his pocket and took out the coin, giving it to their grateful father. Then he went home with a heart full of joy to what he imagined would be his last meal for many days.

The next morning, though, Hudson received a letter with a blurred postmark. He didn't recognize the handwriting. When he opened the envelope, out fell a coin that was worth four times as much as the one he had given away. There was no letter and Hudson never did find out where it came from. It was just enough money to tide him over until his rent was due.

Two weeks later, Hudson got on his knees again and prayed that God would supply the money he needed for his landlady. Hudson did not want her to suffer because of his decision to live by faith. When Dr. Hardey delayed paying him yet again, Hudson prayed until he felt sure that God would meet his need some other way. He remained in his room, praying and thanking God for the answer in faith.

Late that evening, Dr. Hardey came up the stairs to Hudson's apartment, laughing heartily. "Here, take this money," he told Hudson. "A former patient just arrived at my door and paid his bill in full. He must be crazy to come so late with money on a Sunday! Keep whatever I owe you."

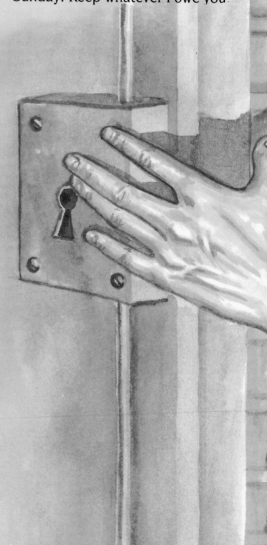

THE GOLDEN OPPORTUNITY

During the following years Hudson became more and more determined to move closer to his dream of going to China. He turned down offers of money toward his studies, showing he cared more about getting a stronger faith than getting a strong education. He chose to live on brown bread and water. "I want to practice what I preach," he wrote in his journal. "My goal is to move men and women to God through prayer alone." Besides, time is running out, he thought. If I wait until I've become a doctor to sail for China, millions will have perished without knowing Jesus. I must pray for an opportunity soon.

Then one day, the opportunity Hudson had been waiting for arrived. Leaders of the rebellion in China had gotten the upper hand in the war and were showing an openness to western ideas. Hudson heard they wanted Christian teachers in Shanghai and knew his golden moment had arrived. It may be now or never. The door is open and I must go through it, he determined.

Although Hudson had no medical degree, university training or papers of ordination, he did have the enthusiasm and courage of ten men as he made plans to sail away. With the promise of financial sponsorship from the Chinese Evangelization Society in London, Hudson stored away medicines and doctor's instruments alongside Chinese Bibles and books, wrapping everything carefully for the four-month voyage. With bags and boxes in tow, he left his family on the dock in Liverpool, England and turned his vision toward the East.

DUMFRIES

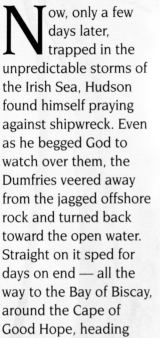

Now, only a few days later, trapped in the unpredictable storms of the Irish Sea, Hudson found himself praying against shipwreck. Even as he begged God to watch over them, the Dumfries veered away from the jagged offshore rock and turned back toward the open water. Straight on it sped for days on end — all the way to the Bay of Biscay, around the Cape of Good Hope, heading past Australia and onward, right into the East China Sea.

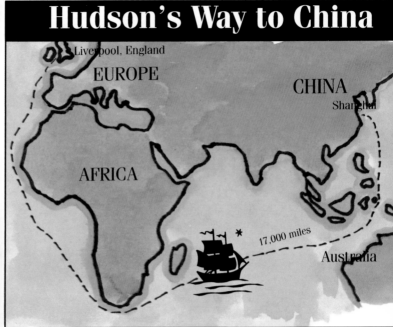

Hudson's Way to China

Liverpool, England

EUROPE

CHINA

Shanghai

AFRICA

17,000 miles

Australia

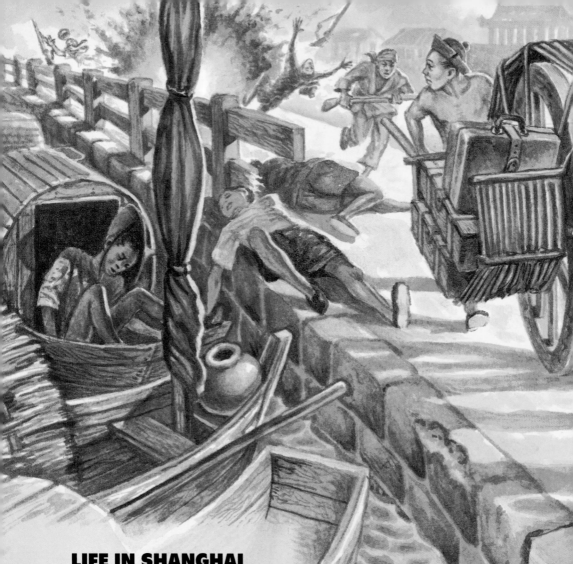

LIFE IN SHANGHAI

When the Dumfries finally docked on an island near the coast of China, Hudson waved goodbye to the crew. He jumped down from the deck onto a small pilot boat headed upriver toward Shanghai. The river's current was steady and serene compared with the slap-dashing sensation of the ocean. Hudson settled back and surveyed his belongings. He had enough supplies to start a medical dispensary, plenty of ink and paper for writing, lots of books and a few clothes.

Stepping ashore at Shanghai, Hudson headed in the direction of a distant English flag. The solid earth seemed to rock beneath his feet and his heart pounded wildly. China, at last! The red, white and blue Union Jack flying above the British consulate meant the promise of people who would help him settle in Shanghai. He expected to draw money there from the account of his sponsors, the Chinese Evangelization Society (C.E.S) and pick up a letter of welcome and instruction.

But the only welcome for Hudson was the sound of gunfire and cannon

blasts. Shanghai was completely occupied by soldiers — the rebellion forces — and surrounded by the imperial army of China. Wounded and dead soldiers lay moaning in the streets. Hudson had to step around them. He paused to allow one group to pass — soldiers hauling captives along the stone streets by their hair. They were going to a place of execution. The doomed men cried out in pain and grapped wildly for Hudson's legs as they were being dragged off.

And so Hudson discovered that the country he had waited so long to see was being torn apart by civil war. In the days that followed there would often be political riots in the city. The Chinese mistrusted people from the West. These things made it hard for the missionaries to cut a path into the interior of the country. Little did Hudson know that the war would drag on for another eleven years, hindering his work every step of the way.

On that first day at the consulate, Hudson found no letter of instruction, no money available to him, no contact person with the C.E.S. mission. Turning aside, he faced the glare of battle going on outside city walls. There was no housing other than shacks, and when food was available, it was old and stale and terribly expensive.

Burned- and bombed-out houses lined the walls of the city of Shanghai. Starving children, orphans and beggars shuffled along the alleyways, despite the freezing temperatures. Hungry women stared at him from hovels. An occasional shrill cry from a child shattered the daylight, turning Hudson's bright expectations to darkness. His vision turned to grim determination. Hudson wanted to help these people and bring them hope. He shuddered in the damp, chill air and walked away from the consulate.

After some time, Hudson met a British doctor in a Shanghai hospital

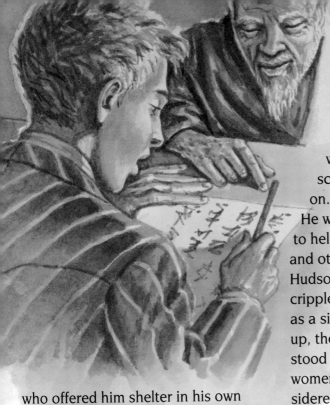

with feet just like hers.

Just then from a house nearby, he heard women's voices crying out, "Stop, stop, please have mercy." The woman on the street pulled a scarf over her head and hurried on. Hudson felt helpless and sad. He wished he could do something to help the women he had just heard and other women in China, as well. Hudson knew many baby girls were crippled on purpose by their families as a sign of wealth. When they grew up, they could barely walk. He understood just how dreadfully most women were treated. They were considered possessions of men, were not allowed to go to school, were sometimes sold as slaves and were often tortured into doing what men wanted them to do. Hudson went home and turned his sadness into prayer for China.

who offered him shelter in his own home. Hudson felt grateful, but frustrated. He ached to get his own place where Bible studies could be held and where he could start a school for the children. Hudson barely knew where to begin. But begin, he did.

Hudson visited shops and offices, made friends with local business people, visited homes where disease and starvation had made entire families sick. He studied Mandarin, the language spoken by most Chinese and got to know other missionaries living in Shanghai.

One evening a woman was shuffling along the street and saw Hudson giving out booklets about Jesus. The woman reached for a booklet, bowed and began to leave. Hudson noticed her feet were so tiny that she could hardly walk. They were the size of a toddler's feet, crippled and deformed. He had seen many women

Not long afterward, Hudson came face to face with the powerful Chinese drug trade. Walking near the harbor, he noticed a large number of boxes containing opium being loaded onto the dock. He learned from other westerners in Shanghai that thousands of pounds of opium were imported into China yearly and used to keep people poor and ignorant through addiction. Wealthy men grew richer from the trade. And the poor were dying. Hudson had always known the powers of darkness and evil cut deep in China. Now he began to realize just how treacherous and dangerous the work was to which God had called him.

Hudson also witnessed the horror of the "coolie traffic" and his heart broke with sadness. One morning he noticed Chinese men being loaded on board a ship by the hundreds. Some were bound and blindfolded, others

appeared to go willingly, but once on board, became confused. The men were refused the right to get off the ship. Hudson heard the crack of whips and moans of pain from men inside the ship's hold. He learned the men were being sent to far-off places to do menial, back-breaking labor and that many would die on the way, while those who did survive the inhumane treatment would never return to China.

Hudson renewed his determination to pray for the Chinese people even as he renewed his commitment to God. He knew there were millions of people sold into slavery from the interior of China. He vowed to be their messenger of salvation. He vowed to challenge other young people in England to respond to the incredible needs in China and bring the freedom of Christ to Chinese people beyond the coastline.

Testaments and thousands of leaflets about the Gospel onto a junk and take off through the narrow, watery passageways. He passed out tracts wherever the boat stopped and took time to explain the message to people for whom it was strange and unbelievable. He realized, also, how odd he must look to these people in his tattered western clothes, fair hair and blue eyes. Most of them stared and gawked at him. Sometimes they ran from him. Other times, they threatened to kill him.

On one trip with a friend, he offered free medical care to the people he met. He soon learned that the potions, pills and powders in his medicine chest fascinated the Chinese and opened a door for his preaching about the salvation God offers through Jesus. Day in and day out, Hudson traveled the waterways leading into the interior of China. This was the land of his dreams. Regardless of how dangerous the trips sometimes were, he felt fulfilled and joyful.

THE DREAM TO REACH INLAND CHINA

Hudson studied the areas on his map north, south and west of Shanghai. These were large, heavily populated regions, linked by an intricate web of waterways. Junks, or small sailboats were readily available to navigate these channels, although Hudson knew travel would be slow and primitive.

Yet the day did come when he could load hundreds of New

Christianity i

One day after many trips, Hudson had an idea. Why not live permanently on a boat? he wondered. Many Chinese do it. Why not live as closely to their lifestyle as possible? I don't want them to notice me because I am a foreigner, but to listen to the stories I have to tell from the Bible. That way I can avoid the suspicions of many who believe I am a spy for the rebellion in China, and I can become better friends with the Chinese wherever I go.

Hudson knew of no other missionaries who had dared to think like this or dared to dress like the Chinese. Though he was certain to be criticized by other westerners, he decided that the acceptance of the Chinese people was more important than that of fellow missionaries. Hudson ordered a pair of wide, short trousers and a silk jacket from a Chinese tailor. He was fitted for a pair of turned-up shoes by a shoemaker. Then he dyed his hair black with the help of a barber and purchased a long braided pigtail hairpiece to wear until his own hair grew long. The next day he appeared dressed as a typical Chinese teacher, a man who would be respected for his education.

Hudson sailed for Tsung-ming where more than one million Chinese lived. The people of Tsung-ming received him with great enthusiasm and curiosity. One of them offered him a room in the attic of a Buddhist temple. Hudson began treating sick people and holding church meetings. It was a confirmation to him that the real work in the interior of China had begun.

...ina

Christianity came to China during the late Middle Ages. But not until today, 600 years later, is it bearing fruit – thanks to Hudson Taylor and many other faithful missionaries who shared the Gospel with the Chinese.

When the atheistic Communists took over in 1949, all western missionaries were thrown out of China, leaving behind an estimat-
Caption: Believers worshipping in house church
ed 900,000 Chinese believers, who were then harassed and persecuted by Communist officials. During the Cultural Revolution (1966-1970) pastors were imprisoned, churches and temples were closed, and religion banned.

But religion survived in the hearts of the Chinese people, and the government eventually allowed Christians to meet in the government-regulated "open" churches. Yet many Christians preferred to worship without being registered and controlled by the government. Underground "house churches" sprang up all over the country. These churches – mainly growing in the rural areas where eighty per cent of the population lives – are self-supporting and self-propagating. A typical house church has 100-300 members who meet in homes at unusual hours so as to avoid harassment by the police. Most members do not even have a Bible. All they have are handwritten copies of Scripture verses. But they are happy and thankful for having been found worthy to suffer for Christ.

Today, an estimated forty million believers meet in house churches, while only six million are affiliated with the official Church.

Despite this early success, Hudson was later forced to return to Shanghai to live. There he continued the inland ministry through frequent trips. Yet on each trip, obstacle after obstacle was placed in his way. His path to the heart of China was blocked again and again by the civil war, diplomatic bureaucracy between Britain and China, threats to his life and the destruction of his medical supplies and books.

One day on a journey by ship from Shanghai to Ningbo, Hudson took along a Chinese man named Peter who had been educated in England. They had become friends and

Hudson often talked to Peter about God. Late that afternoon, Hudson heard a splash and a shout. Peter had fallen overboard and the boatman was pointing to the dark place in the water where he had disappeared.

Hudson jumped over the side of the ship and swam back to the spot, searching desperately in the murky water for Peter. When he saw some nearby fishermen with a dragnet he shouted, "Come and bring that net here! A man is drowning!"

"Not right now," they shouted back. "We're busy fishing. Maybe later."

"I'll pay you well!" answered

Hudson. "Don't wait until it is too late!"

"We won't come for less than thirty coins," the fishermen replied.

"I'll give you everything I have. But hurry!"

Finally, the fishermen brought the net over and within a few minutes hauled Peter to the surface. Hudson tried to revive him, but failed. The loss of time caused by the fishermen's indifference had cost Peter his life.

Hudson was heartsick. They could easily have saved him. But they were too busy. What about the millions of Chinese people dying every day because Christians are distracted by other things? Hudson wondered. Isn't the soul more valuable than the body? I will preach the Gospel every day to as many as I can reach.

Though provisions from England were slow in coming and Hudson often had to go without food, booklets or medicine, he preached at every opportunity and created ways of interesting people in the Gospel. Through every problem, he learned to rest in God, growing daily in love for the Chinese people, even as he had loved Peter.

HUDSON'S LOVE STORY

Months later, hostilities arose between England and China. War broke out between the two countries. Hudson was detained at the town of Ningbo due to the nearby sea battles. While living there, he became acquainted with two young women who were sisters, orphaned as children, now helping to run the first-ever school for girls in China. The girls' parents had been among the earliest missionaries in the country.

The eldest sister, Maria, also participated in neighborhood evangelism. Because of her vision and compassion for the Chinese people and her gentle spirit, Hudson fell in love with Maria. Their friendship blos-

somed until circumstances of war forced an end to it: A plot to massacre all foreigners was discovered in Ningbo and Hudson was chosen to escort families with small children safely back to Shanghai.

Before leaving, Hudson agonized over whether or not to ask for Maria's hand in marriage. What do I have to offer a wife? he asked himself. I can give her no security whatsoever. My funding comes from a weak and disorganized mission society. I've never been able to depend on them. My life is dangerous and physically hard. Why, I haven't even a home or a bed to call my own. I'm always moving about and often criticized by the other missionaries because of my Chinese dress. No, I cannot ask Maria to marry me.

Back in Shanghai, Hudson was almost too busy to miss Maria. Because of the fighting, thousands of homeless refugees poured into the city from outlying districts. Many lived in cemeteries where they took shelter by breaking into the low, arched tombs. Others crowded into ruined buildings. Hudson went on daily rounds to these places, caring for the sick, starving and freezing people. Because of the deteriorating financial situation of the C.E.S., he decided to end his connection with them completely. He took on the status of an independent missionary, trusting in God alone for the food, shelter and provisions he would need. This was unheard of among the missionaries of his time, but Hudson was willing to endure their criticism for the sake of what God had called him to do in China.

In spite of the chaos in Shanghai and the burdens of his work there, Hudson could still not get his mind off the lovely Maria. And back in Ningbo, Maria could not get her mind off Hudson. She was attracted by his commitment to the Chinese people and his willingness to be dependent on God alone. She admired the manner in which he had adopted the Chinese dress and his vision of taking the Gospel to the interior of China.

But Maria was not allowed to communicate with Hudson, so she took all her dreams and desires to God.

At last Hudson sent a letter to Maria declaring his desire to marry her. Maria took the letter to her guardian who responded, "What? How dare that poor, unconnected nobody ask for your hand in marriage? The proposal must be refused at once!" Then she forced poor Maria to write the refusal in her own hand. Maria believed she would never see Hudson again.

But in the spring, Hudson returned to Ningbo on business. Maria's guardian criticized his clothing and scorned his radical dependence on himself and God. She refused to allow him to see Maria. Then a friend of Maria's quietly arranged for a secret meeting between the two young people. Maria and Hudson shared their feelings for each other and agreed to seek God on the matter of marriage.

Hudson told Maria, "If we marry, our life will be difficult. Even now my finances are dwindling to almost nothing. And my calling is dangerous. I'm going to take the gospel further and further into the interior of China."

"Have you forgotten?" Maria replied. "I was left an orphan in a far-off land. God has been my Father all these years; do you think I shall be afraid to trust Him now?"

With confidence in a shared vision, Hudson asked Maria to write for permission to marry from her uncle back in England. Four months later, a letter arrived granting permission. Maria's uncle had been assured from mission associates in London that Hudson was a missionary of unusual promise.

Hudson's marriage with Maria seemed destined to bring closer their mutual vision of reaching inland China, despite the political storms raging around them. The summer of their wedding the Treaty of Tianjin opened the way for foreigners to all interior provinces. The Taylors rejoiced, but decided that next year to stay in Ningbo, rather than move on. This was because the hospital and dispensary there appeared ready to close when the resident physician lost his wife and returned to England with their children. Hudson and Maria accepted the challenge of running the hospital.

Hudson, not sponsored by any medical or missionary society, knew they would have to pray for the funds needed to keep the hospital running. The situation was not new to Hudson. He had been living by faith alone for years and he believed God was with them. Finally, the day came when the last bag of rice had been opened and was disappearing fast as the patients received their daily meal.

Hudson looked at the few grains of rice in the hospital kitchen and said, "The Lord's time for helping us must be close at hand."

Before the end of that day the Taylors had received a check enclosed with a letter from a man they'd never met. "I've inherited a great deal of money," the letter said. "And I prayed about what God would have me do with it. I'm sending it to you in case you may have need of it and will send more if you allow."

"Suppose," Hudson said to Maria, "we had turned down the challenge to take over the hospital because of lack of finances? Or because of lack of faith?"

"Now we can go on helping people here and sharing the Gospel with them," Maria added.

Hudson and Maria threw themselves into the hospital work. But the stress and strain of the project, as well as having to look after their new baby, took its toll on their health and spirits. There was simply too much to do and not enough people to help. They worked hard for six years as patients continued to flood the wards. At last, the endless needs of helpless people finally became too much to bear. Hudson became sick and grew weak. Maria was caring for him and their daughter while performing the administrative duties of the hospital. She was desperate for help. And no help came.

Faced with the impossibility of all she and Hudson were attempting, the day finally came when she closed the door to the Ningbo hospital, giving the large iron key an extra twist. Then she joined Hudson and Gracie on board a ship, and the family headed back to England. Hudson and Maria had come to realize that they must dream a new dream. They talked of stirring interest in British young people to consider service in China. Maria looked forward to a period of rest for herself and hoped Hudson could recover completely from his ill-

ness. They envisioned a time when they would return to their beloved China with plenty of workers to share their vision of reaching the interior.

But doctors in England told Hudson he would never again be strong enough for missionary service. They warned him to slow down and stay put. Year after year they treated him and watched for his health to improve. But Hudson did not listen to his doctors. He was determined to help the Chinese even from his room, which overlooked a dreary street on London's east side.

Hudson worked on a revision of the Chinese New Testament that could be understood by less-educated people. He wrote articles about China from his bed and whenever possible, he called meetings and preached to the English people about the great need in China. Determined to return one day himself, he resumed his medical studies so he would be better prepared to help the Chinese people.

Maria was also busy, giving birth to a son every other year during their stay in England. And she was making the difficult adjustment to what was for her, a strange culture. Maria longed for her childhood home of China and an opportunity to serve its people. Both she and Hudson were homesick for the country they loved half a world away. Their apartment, the British Isles and traditions there, all seemed too small for their vision and dreams.

Hudson was discouraged that men and women were not responding to the call of need in China. The flurry of interest stirred by his arrival in London had now died down. "God has put me on a shelf," he said to Maria.

But every day Hudson studied a map of China and prayed for inland areas by name and the people he knew who had responded to the Gospel message in each place. Hudson compiled facts about the size and population of every province. One day he got a letter from a mission society in England: "The number

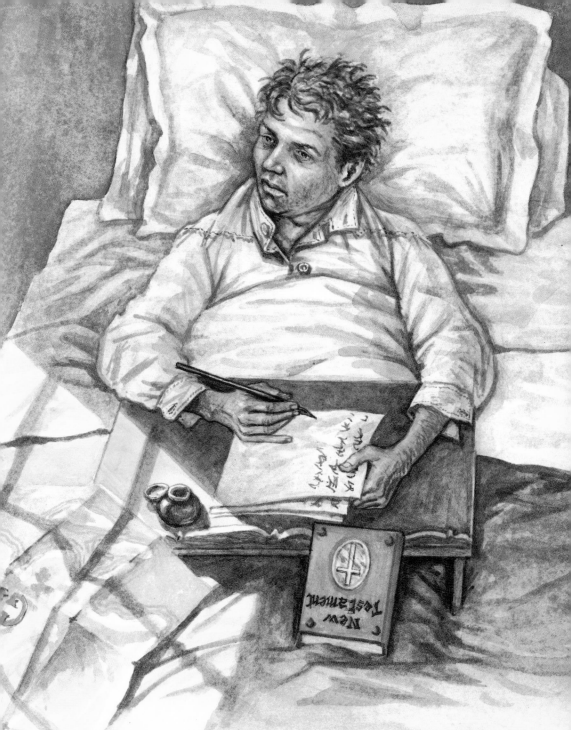

of Protestant missionaries in China has been reduced from 115 to 91 in recent months," it reported. Hudson grieved at the loss of workers. People are perishing daily and we in England are allowing it to happen, he thought. We are too busy attending to our own affairs to be concerned about men drowning in a sea of spiritual darkness. Then he thought of his friend Peter. Hudson became so sad, he ceased to write in his journal for seven weeks. He just sat alone and prayed and cried.

Finally, one day Hudson took a walk on the beach. He felt alone, exhausted and thoroughly spent from his grief. As the waves beat the shoreline, he stopped speaking to God and started listening.

"Seek from Me the needed workers," the Lord told him. "Stop trying to do it all yourself. Pray for the spiritual life of the Church so that out of it, young people will respond. Trust Me."

"But Lord," Hudson replied, "What if new workers come, but fail? We need at least twenty-four, two for each of the eleven provinces without a missionary and two for Mongolia. But I can't offer them any security at all — only danger and life on the brink of starvation. What if they break down under the burden? What if they can't endure the political problems? What if they are not up to it?"

"The power," said God, "by which I call men and women will also be the power by which I keep them."

"Then, Lord, take the burden off my back," Hudson cried. "I'll leave it up to You."

ered fanatical and rebellious by many churches and mission boards.

"My past experience of God's faithfulness gives me the courage to proceed," Hudson told startled church members who questioned the wisdom of his idea. "I've survived storms at sea, civil war battles, political uprisings and sickness. But from the response of the Chinese people, I know we have a covenant-keeping God."

"That brash upstart!" said one minister when he read of Hudson's idea. "This new mission might take away men or money from already existing organizations! What good will it do in the kingdom of God — robbing Peter to pay Paul?"

A NEW ADVENTURE IN FAITH

Two days later Hudson went to the London and County Bank and opened an account for what he entitled the China Inland Mission (C.I.M.). He deposited ten pounds sterling into the account — every cent he and Maria owned. This would be the start of a new kind of mission society where workers had to trust God alone for food and provision.

"There will be no salaries for outgoing missionaries," he and Maria agreed. "We can afford to have as little as the Lord chooses to give. We will wear native dress and head inland."

Hudson knew the idea of an organization requiring missionaries to go without secure funding and to dress like the native people was a radical idea. He knew he would be consid-

Hudson responded to this criticism even before he had heard of it. He established standards that allowed C.I.M. to accept workers not accepted by other missions, particularly those who hadn't completed university training. No one would be recruited or asked to join the mission.

"We will depend on God alone to prompt those whom He wants to volunteer," Hudson announced. "And we will not appeal for money! In this way we will not divert money from other organizations."

"It is a foolhardy business," snapped Hudson's critics. "It's an impossible idea. You will be forgotten and soon find yourself without even the necessities of life!"

"God is moving," Hudson told them. "Are we willing to move with Him?"

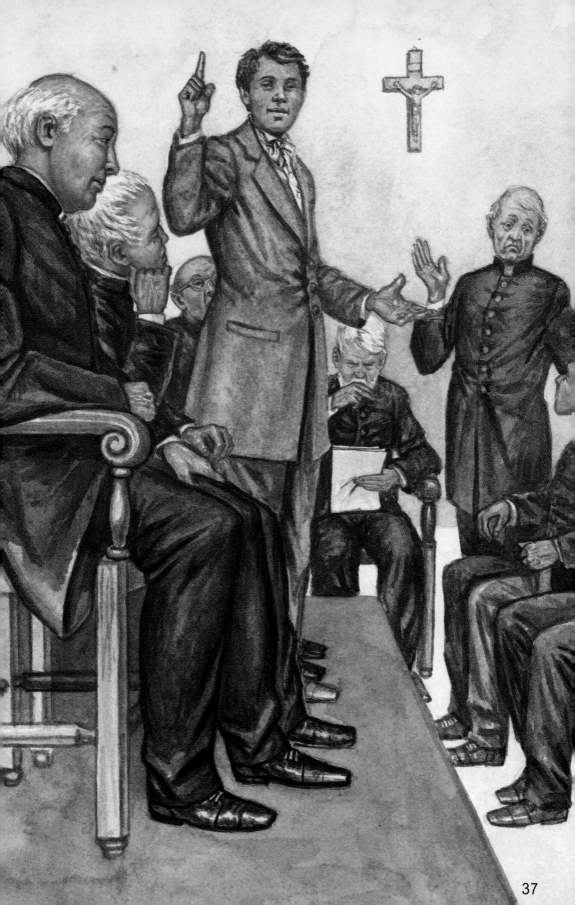

REBIRTH OF A DREAM

Two small boys grasped the hands of their older sister and crossed the gangplank onto a huge ship. As the mast creaked in the breeze they looked up at their mother for assurance. Maria carried their baby brother in one arm and a suitcase in the other. "It's all right boys," she said. "Let's get up on top and then we can see the water." Maria and her oldest child, Gracie, saw the anxiety in the boys' eyes and Gracie squeezed their fingers in hers while Maria prodded them with gentle words.

Hudson followed the family on board the Lammermuir with sixteen missionaries behind them. Volunteer missionaries had responded to the call of the China Inland Mission and had been training and studying Chinese together for months. The excitement and anticipation on their faces was a source of great joy to Hudson. These are God's chosen workers, he thought. And I trust Him to send the final eight workers soon.

The party was ready for the four-month voyage. Maria and Hudson had plenty of help with the children as the young missionaries pitched in with schooling and practical care. After a few weeks at sea, the children settled down and began to enjoy the shifts in the wind and the rocking of the ship. Even though they were heading off to an unknown land, they were secure in the protection of parents who had taught them to trust God and love Him.

40

When the Lammermuir finally reached the China Sea, there was great excitement on board as they neared their destination. Soon they would have real beds, fresh food and be able to walk and run for miles if they wanted. With cramped legs, they stood on deck one night hoping to catch their first sight of land. Suddenly, the air changed, the wind picked up and the sky opened, drenching the ship with rain. Taking refuge in their cabins below, the Taylor family and their friends knelt and prayed.

Day after day, the ship was battered by one typhoon after another. Rain and sleet kept the decks wet. The storms blew the vessel off course and threatened to destroy it. For twelve days, the crew and passengers fought fear, nausea and discouragement. Then one morning, they saw the coast of China. Just as they began to rejoice, another typhoon came along and blew the ship in the opposite direction. It was as if the ship could take no more. The jibs and staysails gave way. The decks were swept by a violent sea. Soon one entire side of the ship had rolled under water. The jibboom broke, followed by the foretop and masts. They swung in the wind like broken arms on a worn-out doll. Tubs, buckets, cask and timbers floated all around the little ship.

The captain ordered everyone to put on life belts. "The ship can scarcely hold together for another two hours," he said. "We're going under."

Hudson kissed his children in their cabin below, left them in the care of Maria and climbed on deck to join the crew. He found them taking refuge in the forecastle with revolvers, intending to use them on themselves if washed into the sea.

"Please, don't use force," Hudson pleaded. "We must try everything to stay afloat. We must keep working. God will bring us through this, but the navigation depends on you."

All who could, climbed up on deck. Men and women together took turns manning the pumps. They pulled what was left of the damaged sails, working day after day, night after night to keep the ship from the sea. It was an exhausted and ragged group of missionaries who finally landed in a mangled vessel on the coast of China one week later.

When the other Shanghai mission-aries saw them, one man chided, "Hudson Taylor is back. And he's brought six unmarried ladies with him. Imagine bringing unmarried English women to China!"

"Yes, and they say he plans to send them inland!" said another.

"In Chinese dress, no less!" said someone else. "Is this Taylor some sort of madman?"

"Where will they stay?" another wondered. "I've heard they have no financial support from England. How

will they stay alive? They don't even have a place to sleep tonight."

The ragged party immediately boarded houseboats to travel into China's interior toward Hangzhou. They were in search of permanent headquarters for their mission. The nights were bitterly cold and several people became ill. Maria stayed on board the boat and cared for them while Hudson explored the city of Hangzhou for a place to stay and to plan the next step of going further inland.

Before the end of a year in Hangzhou, tragedy struck the small party of missionaries. Winter came and went, and summer arrived with its stifling 103 degree heat. As a result, tempers flared and fighting broke out among the members of the China Inland Mission. Several in the group criticized the dress standards, while others complained about Hudson's leadership style. Worst of all, one day Hudson and Maria's only daughter became sick. Within a few desperate hours, little Gracie was dead.

"She was the sunshine of our lives," Hudson wrote to his sister back in England. "I'll never forget the day we buried her — those little white hands folded on her bosom, holding a single flower. It is too sad."

But Hudson and Maria were determined to pursue their vision. They decided to work harder than ever and put their sadness behind them. They went out preaching and helped the sick as far as they could go up the waterways of inland China. Within a few months, members of the C.I.M. were establishing churches in cities twenty-four days' journey from each other.

The Taylors accepted as part of mission life that wherever they went, there was the possibility of riots against them. In Hangzhou the people who had first welcomed the missionaries now hated them. They passed out papers saying the foreigners who preached "the religion of Jesus" had committed horrible crimes.

One night an angry mob of Chinese people gathered outside the door of the C.I.M., accusing the Taylors of kidnapping Chinese children.

"Revenge!" cried the mob. "Attack! Destroy the foreigners! Take their medicines. Burn their books!"

Hudson crept away in the darkness and raced to the governor's house for help. He slipped through the gates, but was kept waiting as he listened to the rioters' shouts back at the house. He knew Maria and the children were defenseless in the hands of the angry mob. "God must protect us," he prayed. "Lord, You are the only defense we can count on now or ever." And Hudson's family was protected.

HUDSON'S DREAM COMES TRUE

For many years Hudson and Maria continued to work from town to town. There were more riots. Some of the missionaries wanted to give up. Others criticized Hudson for the way he led the mission. It was never easy to find enough food or medicine. The Taylors had to nurse each other and their sons through sickness, loneliness and fear. At one point, before the hot summer season started, they decided to send their four older children back to safety in England because the boys had been so ill and weak.

Then tragedy struck again when shortly before the children were set to sail, one of the boys died. The hardest thing Maria ever did was put the other two on the ship, not knowing whether they would ever see each other again. Although she was determined to do the best for them and for the ministry, staying behind in China without her children nearly broke

Maria's heart. Weakened by that, Maria fell ill with cholera. She was pregnant at the time and her newborn son died shortly after being born. Maria's strength was gone and she died soon afterwards in her husband's arms.

Hudson buried Maria and their infant son beside Gracie and her younger brother. It was a crushing blow. Still, he determined that the work must go on in spite of the pain, and the crippling effect Maria's death had on the ministry. "Perhaps God will give new life out of this death," he hoped.

There were still nine Chinese provinces with no missionaries at all. Getting money to support more workers had always been a problem. Hudson wrote articles about the need in China, challenging Christians to pray. Outside China he spoke wherever he could get an invitation to talk about China. Then one by one, Hudson received applications from eighteen young people who answered the call to come work with the China Inland Mission.

Hudson was not satisfied with temporary missionaries. He wanted to establish permanent mission stations in each of the provinces.

"God will provide the workers and the money," he had always said.

Hudson traveled several times back and forth to England, each time further expanding the work. He eventually married again and his wife took up work among the Chinese women. In the meantime, Hudson began to make visits to America and Europe, always calling for more missionaries. Soon there were a thousand volun-

China Today
A Nation Ripe for Harvest

China is the most densely populated nation on earth, with 1.4 billion people (or almost one-fourth of the world's total population).

After almost fifty years of Communism most Chinese people are disillusioned with their government. In the 1980s, a youthful democratic movement marched forward. But on June 4, 1989, the old Communist rulers crushed the peaceful democrats in a bloody massacre in Tiananmen Square in Beijing. Thousands of students were gunned down.

The Tiananmen massacre quenched any hope of speedy political freedom. Now more and more people are turning to Christianity for spiritual freedom. Ironically, the number of Christians in China now exceeds the number of Communist Party members. Huge numbers of young people are flooding into the house churches – 28,000 every day. At this rate, there will be over 10 million new Christians each year. By the end of this millennium the Christians in China may exceed one billion. And these believers are no nominal Christians – they are Christians on fire for Christ, having suffered and been martyred for Him.

The many ethnic groups in China present a special challenge to the Church of God worldwide. There are fifty-five "national minorities" among the total of ninety-one million people (eight per cent of China's population). The majority of these groups (sixty-five million people) have never heard the Gospel of Jesus Christ – and some of those who have, are still considered among the least evangelized peoples in the world. (One such group, the exiled Tibetans who have been exposed to missionary work for over 150 years, has had only a hundred converts.)

How can western Christians most effectively reach out to their persecuted brothers and sisters in China? First, we can pray that God will raise up mature Chinese leaders and teachers to disciple the new converts. Secondly, we can give financial support to mission organizations, radio broadcasting and literature work. Thirdly, we can go ourselves or send English teachers and other professionals to work in China. The spiritual fields of China are ready for the greatest harvest the world has ever seen.

teers, but Hudson was spending less time in China than he wanted.

At 73, Hudson finally returned to China with his son and daughter-in-law, doing the very work he so loved. Together, they sailed the inland waterways telling people about Jesus. There was barely a city in the interior of China that had not been reached by missionaries whom Hudson had inspired and challenged. Hudson had seen his dream come true.

Main Events in Hudson Taylor's Life

1832 (May 21) Hudson Taylor was born in Barnsley, Yorkshire, England.

1849 (June) Makes personal commitment to Jesus Christ.

1850 (May) Begins medical studies in Hull as assistant to Dr. Robert Hardey.

1853 (September) Sails for China, sponsored by the Chinese Evangelization Society.

1854 (March) Lands in Shanghai.

1850–1864 Taiping Rebellion in China.

1854–1855 Makes ten evangelistic journeys.

1855 (Oct.-Nov.) Makes his first home in "inland" China.

1856 (October) Settles temporarily in Ningbo where he meets Maria Dyer who will become his wife.

1857 (June) Resigns from the Chinese Evangelization Society.

1858 (January) Marries Maria Dyer.

1859 (September) Takes charge, with Maria, of Dr. Parker's hospital in Ningbo.

1860–1865 Becomes ill and returns to England with Maria and daughter Grace. Three sons are born to the family. Hudson is in a spiritual desert. He translates the New Testament into the Ningbo Chinese dialect and attempts to recruit new missionaries for China.

1865 (June) Surrenders his dream to God. He founds the China Inland Mission (C.I.M.) and writes influential book, **China's Spiritual Needs and Claims.**

1866 (May) The Taylor family sails to China with the first 16 volunteers with the China Inland Mission.

1866 (December) The C. I. M. settles in Hangchow, China.

1867 (August) Oldest child, daughter Grace dies.

1868 Survives the riot at Hangzhou. House is rebuilt and another son (their sixth child) is born.

1870 Sends four oldest surviving children back to England; one son (5-year-old Samuel) dies shortly before the trip.

1870 (July) Wife, Maria dies shortly after a newborn son dies.

1871 Returns to England and marries Jenny Faulding, a fellow missionary to China and family friend.

1872 (August) Forms the London Council of the C.I.M.

1872 (October) Return to China with Jenny, the second Mrs. Taylor.

1874–1875 Is injured and returns to England; develops paralysis. Appeals for prayer for 18 pioneer missionaries for the nine unevangelized provinces.

1876–1878 Widespread evangelistic journeys throughout inland China.

1878 (autumn) Jenny Taylor leads women missionaries far into the interior of China.

1888 (summer) Hudson's first visit to North America to appeal for volunteer workers to China.

1889 (November) Visits Sweden, Norway and Denmark.

1890 (August) Visits Australia.

1900 (May) Beginning of the Boxer Rebellion where foreigners were expelled.

1901 Retires leadership of C.I.M. Eight hundred missionaries representing several denominations — nearly half of the evangelical missionaries in China— are with the C.I.M.

1904 (July) Jenny Taylor dies in Switzerland.

1905 (February) Hudson returns to China for the last time.

1905 (June 3) Hudson Taylor dies in China.

HUDSON TAYLOR'S CHINA

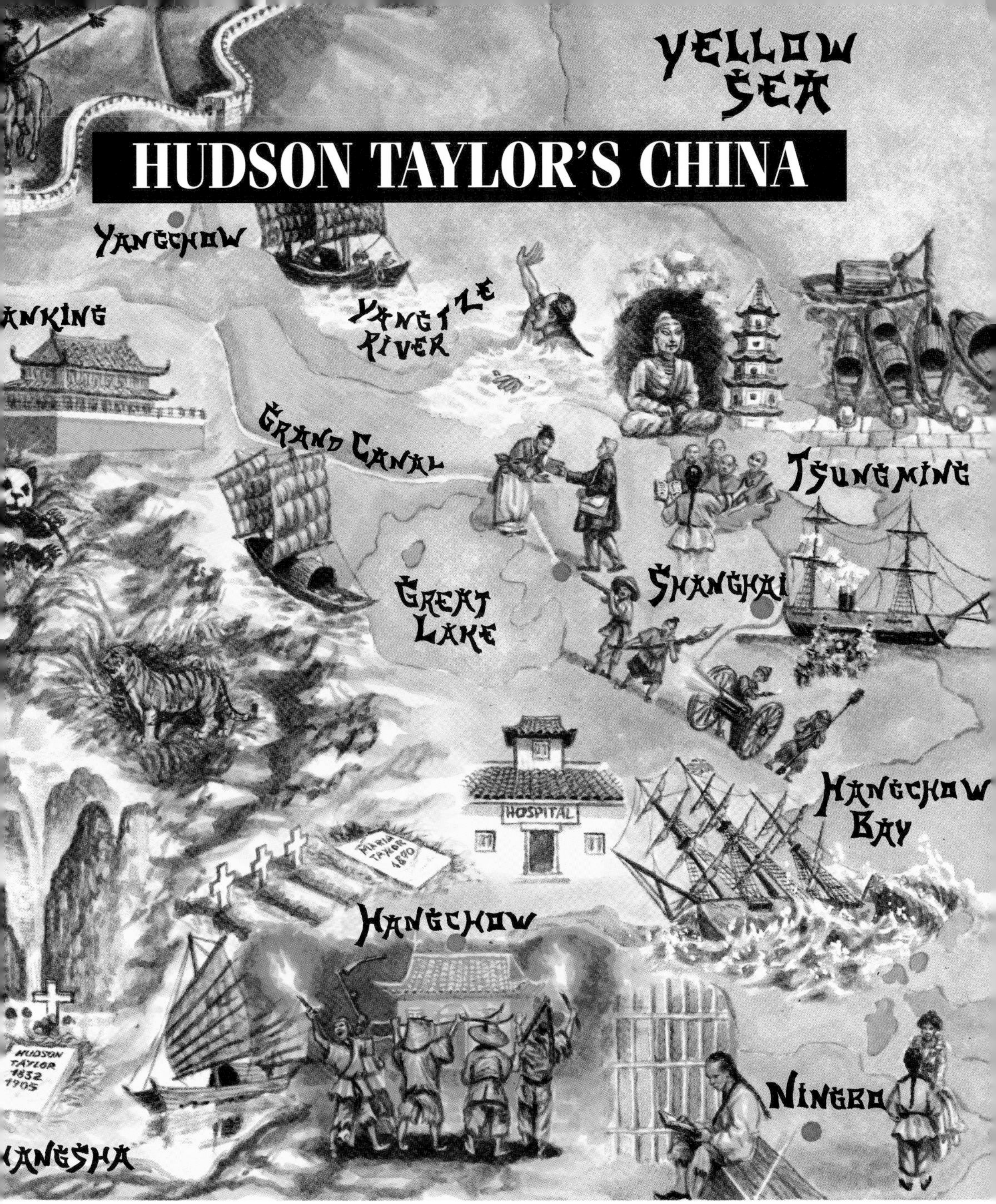

(Map labels) YELLOW SEA · YANGCHOW · NANKING · YANGTZE RIVER · GRAND CANAL · GREAT LAKE · TSUNGMING · SHANGHAI · HANGCHOW BAY · HOSPITAL · MARIA TAYLOR 1890 · HANGCHOW · HUDSON TAYLOR 1832 1905 · NINGBO · CHANGSHA

BOOK RESOURCES

Hudson Taylor's Spiritual Secret, by Dr. and Mrs. Howard Taylor (Discovery House Publishers, 1990).

J. Hudson Taylor: A Man in Christ, by Roger Steer (Harold Shaw Publishers, 1990).

God's Adventurer, by Phyllis Thompson (Overseas Missionary Fellowship, 1991).

Hudson Taylor, by J. Hudson Taylor (Bethany House Publishers, 1991).

Shanghaied to China, by Dave and Neta Jackson (Bethany House Publishers, 1993).

Hudson Taylor, by Susan Martins Miller (Barbour and Company, 1993).

The Church in China, by Carl Lawrence (Bethany House Publishers, 1985).